Bike
Watching
An Explorer's Journal

Bikes

BIANCHI

COLNAGO MASTER

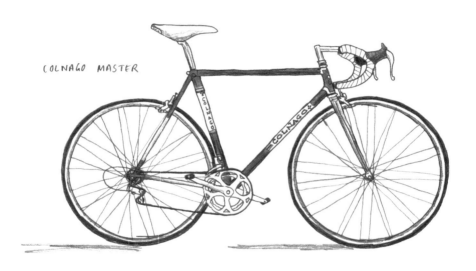

EDDY MERCKX
MOTOROLA
TEAM ISSUE

FLYING
GATE

PARIS
GALIBIER

MOULTON

CERVELO S1

CURVY LO-PRO

FIXIE

MOTOBECANE MIXTE

TANDEM

TRICYCLE

DUTCH BIKE

PENNY FARTHING

Sightings

4   Make/Model: *Bianchi*

Date:

Location:

6   Make/Model:

Date:

Location:

8   Make/Model: *Colnago Master*

Date:

Location:

10   Make/Model:

Date:

Location:

12   Make/Model: *Eddy Merckx Motorola*

Date:

Location:

14   Make/Model:

Date:

Location:

16   Make/Model: *Flying Gate*

Date:

Location:

18   Make/Model:

Date:

Location:

20   Make/Model: *Paris Galibier*

Date:

Location:

22   Make/Model:

Date:

Location:

24 Make/Model: *Moulton*

Date:

Location:

26 Make/Model:

Date:

Location:

28 Make/Model: *Cervélo S1*

Date:

Location:

30 Make/Model:

Date:

Location:

32 Make/Model: *Curvy Lo-pro*

Date:

Location:

34 Make/Model:

Date:

Location:

36 Make/Model: *Fixie*

Date:

Location:

38 Make/Model:

Date:

Location:

40 Make/Model: *Motobecane Mixte*

Date:

Location:

42 Make/Model:

Date:

Location:

44 Make/Model: *Tandem*

Date:

Location:

46 Make/Model:

Date:

Location:

48 Make/Model: *Tricycle*

Date:

Location:

50 Make/Model:

Date:

Location:

52 Make/Model: *Dutch Bike*

Date:

Location:

54 Make/Model:

Date:

Location:

56 Make/Model: *Penny Farthing*

Date:

Location:

58 Make/Model:

Date:

Location:

Accessories

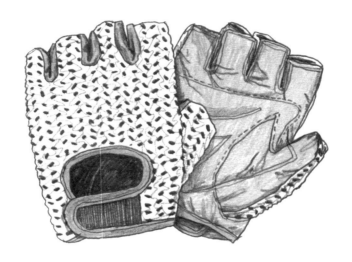

Sightings

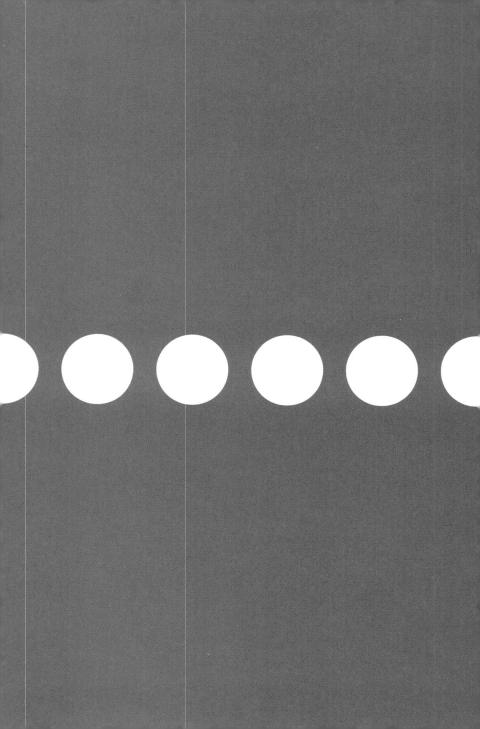

Components

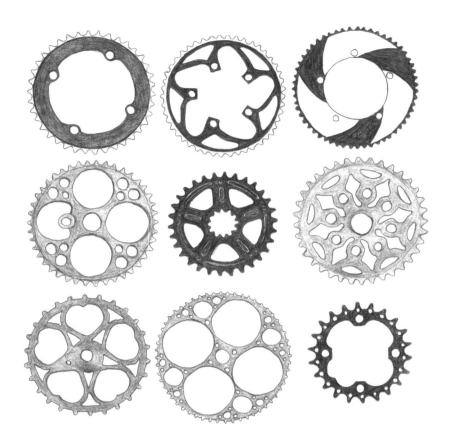

SHIMANO DURA-ACE

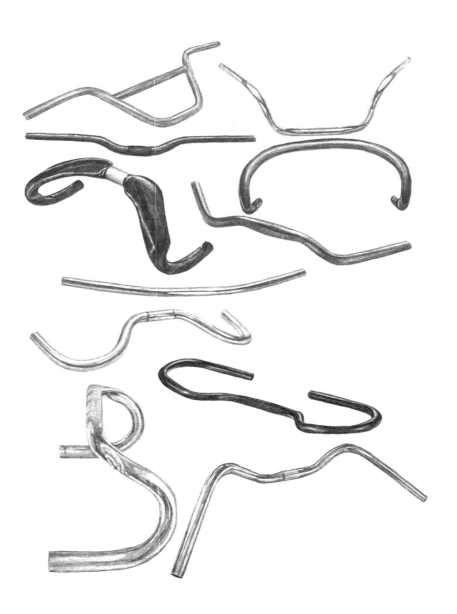

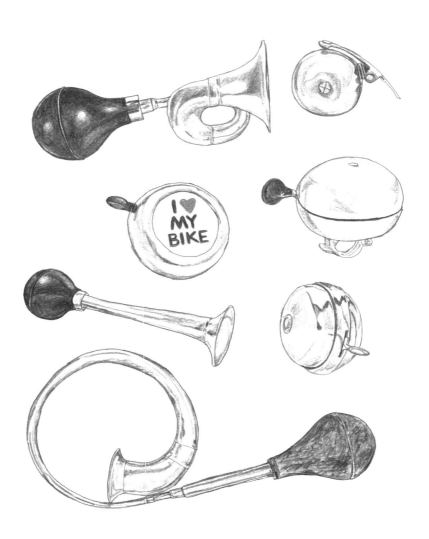

BROOKS B-17

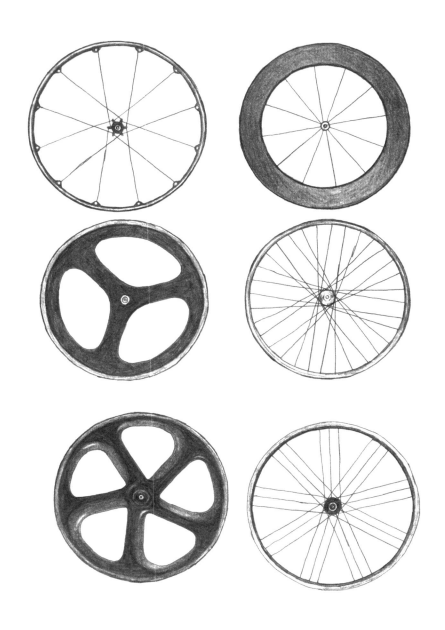

Sightings

Events

CRITICAL MASS

Sightings

114　Event: *Bike Polo*

　　Details: _____

　　Date: _____

　　Location: _____

116　Event: _____

　　Details: _____

　　Date: _____

　　Location: _____

118　Event: *BMX Race*

　　Details: _____

　　Date: _____

　　Location: _____

120　Event: _____

　　Details: _____

　　Date: _____

　　Location: _____

122　Event: *Club Ride*

　　Details: _____

　　Date: _____

　　Location: _____

124　Event: _____

　　Details: _____

　　Date: _____

　　Location: _____

126　Event: *Critical Mass*

　　Details: _____

　　Date: _____

　　Location: _____

128　Event: _____

　　Details: _____

　　Date: _____

　　Location: _____

130　Event: *Tour de France, Mountain Stage*

　　Details: _____

　　Date: _____

　　Location: _____

132　Event: _____

　　Details: _____

　　Date: _____

　　Location: _____

134　Event: *Tweed Run*

　　Details: _____

　　Date: _____

　　Location: _____

Observations

HIRE BIKE

Sightings

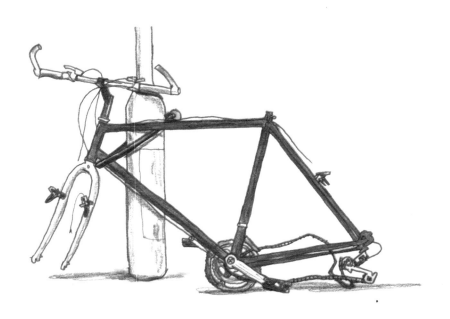

Illustrations © 2012 David Sparshott
Bike consultant: Max Leonard
Design by Struktur Design
ISBN: 978-1-85669-918-1
Printed in China
Magma for Laurence King
www.laurenceking.com

LAURENCE KING